CAN YOU RUN YOUR GAS CAR ON WATER?

Can You Run Your Gas Car on Water?

Walter the Educator

Silent King Books
A WhichHead Entertainment Imprint

Copyright © 2024 by Walter the Educator

All rights reserved. No part of this book may be reproduced in any manner whatsoever without written permission except in the case of brief quotations embodied in critical articles and reviews.

First Printing, 2024

Disclaimer

The author and publisher offer this information without warranties expressed or implied. No matter the grounds, neither the author nor the publisher will be accountable for any losses, injuries, or other damages caused by the reader's use of this book. Your use of this book acknowledges an understanding and acceptance of this disclaimer.

Can You Run Your Gas Car on Water is a little problem solver book by Walter the Educator that belongs to the Little Problem Solver Books Series.
Collect them all and more books at WaltertheEducator.com

LITTLE PROBLEM SOLVER BOOKS

INTRO

In the quest to reduce reliance on fossil fuels and decrease carbon emissions, there has been a resurgence of interest in alternative fuels. One idea that has captivated the imagination of both enthusiasts and skeptics is the possibility of running gas-powered vehicles on water. This concept is commonly linked to "water fuel" systems or the more specific idea of using water (H_2O) to generate hydrogen gas (H_2), which can then be used as a supplemental or even primary fuel for an internal combustion engine. But can you truly run your gas car on water? The answer is more complex than a simple yes or no, and it involves an understanding of chemistry, engineering, and some of the limitations of current technologies.

This little book explores how water can theoretically be used in a car, the challenges involved, and whether this technology is viable for mainstream use.

Can You Run Your Gas Car on Water?

The Concept behind Running a Car on Water

At the heart of the idea of running a car on water is the process of electrolysis, which involves splitting water into hydrogen and oxygen gases. Water, as you know, is composed of two hydrogen atoms and one oxygen atom (H_2O). Hydrogen is an energy-dense gas that can be used as fuel in various applications, including in cars.

Can You Run Your Gas Car on Water?

The principle behind using water as fuel is not to burn water itself but to extract the hydrogen from it. This can then be used to supplement or replace gasoline in powering the internal combustion engine.

Can You Run Your Gas Car on Water?

The primary method proposed for this is the use of an on-board electrolysis system, which would split water into its hydrogen and oxygen components. The hydrogen gas would then be fed into the engine as a fuel, or in some systems, it could be mixed with the air intake, enriching the combustion process. This, in turn, could theoretically reduce the amount of gasoline needed and improve fuel efficiency. Let's break down how this process is supposed to work.

Can You Run Your Gas Car on Water?

1. Electrolysis of Water

Electrolysis is a well-known chemical process used to break water (H_2O) into its constituent elements, hydrogen (H_2) and oxygen (O_2). This process requires an electric current, which, in theory, can be supplied by the car's electrical system, such as the alternator or battery. When water undergoes electrolysis, the following simple overall reaction occurs:

Can You Run Your Gas Car on Water?

$$2H_2O(l) \rightarrow O_2(g) + 2H_2(g)$$

This reaction yields hydrogen gas and oxygen gas. The hydrogen can be used as a fuel for the engine, while the oxygen is a by-product.

Can You Run Your Gas Car on Water?

However, one of the most important points to understand is that electrolysis requires a significant amount of energy. The energy required to split water into hydrogen and oxygen is substantial, and this energy typically needs to come from an external source. For a car, this energy would come from the vehicle's alternator or battery.

Can You Run Your Gas Car on Water?

The alternator is powered by the engine, which uses gasoline, creating a paradox. The energy required to produce hydrogen is higher than the energy gained from burning the hydrogen, leading to inefficiencies.

Can You Run Your Gas Car on Water?

2. Hydrogen as a Fuel

Hydrogen is a highly flammable and energy-dense gas, making it an excellent fuel. When hydrogen combusts in the presence of oxygen, it produces water vapor and releases a significant amount of energy. The combustion of hydrogen can be represented as:

Can You Run Your Gas Car on Water?

$O_2(g) + 2H_2(g) \rightarrow 2H_2O(g)$

The appeal of using hydrogen as a fuel lies in its clean combustion process. Unlike gasoline, which emits carbon dioxide (CO_2), nitrogen oxides (NO_x), and other pollutants, hydrogen only emits water vapor, making it an environmentally friendly alternative.

Can You Run Your Gas Car on Water?

In theory, supplementing gasoline with hydrogen could improve the overall efficiency of the engine by allowing it to use less fuel. Additionally, since hydrogen burns more cleanly than gasoline, it could reduce the emissions produced by the car. However, as promising as this sounds, there are several challenges that need to be considered.

Can You Run Your Gas Car on Water?

Challenges and Limitations

While the idea of using water to produce hydrogen fuel for cars is theoretically possible, there are significant challenges and limitations that make this approach difficult to implement in practice.

Can You Run Your Gas Car on Water?

1. Energy Efficiency

The first and most significant challenge is energy efficiency. The process of electrolysis is inherently inefficient. In fact, it requires more energy to produce hydrogen from water than the hydrogen will provide when burned as fuel.

Can You Run Your Gas Car on Water?

This is due to the laws of thermodynamics, specifically the principle that energy cannot be created or destroyed, only transformed. In this case, the electrical energy required to split water into hydrogen and oxygen is greater than the chemical energy that can be recovered from burning the hydrogen.

Can You Run Your Gas Car on Water?

This inefficiency means that the car's engine would have to work harder, and burn more gasoline, to power the alternator and produce the hydrogen. As a result, the car could end up using more fuel overall, negating any potential benefits of using hydrogen as a supplemental fuel.

Can You Run Your Gas Car on Water?

2. Hydrogen Storage and Safety

Another significant challenge is the storage and handling of hydrogen. Hydrogen is a highly flammable gas, and storing it safely in a vehicle requires specialized equipment.

Can You Run Your Gas Car on Water?

\

While small amounts of hydrogen can be produced on demand through electrolysis, storing larger quantities of hydrogen for use as a primary fuel requires pressurized tanks or cryogenic storage systems.

Can You Run Your Gas Car on Water?

These systems are expensive, complex, and potentially dangerous. A hydrogen leak in a car could pose a serious safety risk, as hydrogen is highly explosive when mixed with air.

Can You Run Your Gas Car on Water?

Additionally, the infrastructure for refueling with hydrogen is not widely available, meaning that a car running on hydrogen would be limited in terms of where it could be refueled.

Can You Run Your Gas Car on Water?

3. Cost and Complexity

The cost of implementing a water-to-hydrogen fuel system in a car is another major hurdle. The equipment required for electrolysis, hydrogen storage, and engine modifications is expensive.

Can You Run Your Gas Car on Water?

Additionally, the system would need to be carefully designed and engineered to ensure that it works safely and efficiently. This adds to the complexity of the vehicle and increases the likelihood of maintenance issues.

Can You Run Your Gas Car on Water?

While some aftermarket kits claim to offer the ability to convert a car to run on water or hydrogen, these kits are often unreliable and may not provide the performance or efficiency improvements they promise.

Can You Run Your Gas Car on Water?

In many cases, these systems end up being more trouble than they are worth, requiring constant maintenance and adjustment to keep them running properly.

Can You Run Your Gas Car on Water?

4. Legal and Regulatory Issues

Even if it were technically possible to run a car on water by using hydrogen, there are legal and regulatory issues to consider.

Can You Run Your Gas Car on Water?

Automotive manufacturers are required to meet strict emissions standards, and any modifications to a vehicle's fuel system must comply with these regulations. In many countries, modifying a car to run on hydrogen or water could void its warranty and make it illegal to drive on public roads.

Can You Run Your Gas Car on Water?

Additionally, there are concerns about the environmental impact of hydrogen production. While hydrogen itself is a clean fuel, the process of producing hydrogen from water can generate carbon emissions if the electricity used for electrolysis comes from fossil fuels.

Can You Run Your Gas Car on Water?

To truly be an environmentally friendly option, the electricity for electrolysis would need to come from renewable sources such as solar or wind power.

Can You Run Your Gas Car on Water?

Practical Alternatives to Running a Car on Water

While the concept of running a car on water presents significant challenges, there are practical alternatives that achieve similar goals of reducing fuel consumption and emissions. These include hybrid vehicles, hydrogen fuel cells, and electric vehicles.

Can You Run Your Gas Car on Water?

1. Hybrid Vehicles

Hybrid vehicles combine a gasoline engine with an electric motor and battery. The electric motor provides additional power to supplement the gasoline engine, reducing the overall amount of fuel consumed.

Can You Run Your Gas Car on Water?

Hybrid vehicles are a proven technology and are widely available, offering significant improvements in fuel efficiency and emissions without the complexity of hydrogen or water fuel systems.

Can You Run Your Gas Car on Water?

2. Hydrogen Fuel Cells

While running a car on hydrogen gas through combustion is inefficient, hydrogen fuel cells offer a more promising alternative. A hydrogen fuel cell generates electricity by combining hydrogen with oxygen in a chemical reaction. This electricity can then be used to power an electric motor, providing a clean and efficient way to use hydrogen as a fuel.

Can You Run Your Gas Car on Water?

Hydrogen fuel cell vehicles are already available in some markets, although they face challenges in terms of cost, infrastructure, and hydrogen production. Nevertheless, they offer a viable path forward for using hydrogen as a clean fuel for transportation.

Can You Run Your Gas Car on Water?

3. Electric Vehicles

Electric vehicles (EVs) represent the most practical and scalable alternative to gasoline-powered cars. EVs are powered by electricity stored in batteries, which can be charged from the electrical grid. When the electricity comes from renewable sources such as solar or wind power, EVs offer a zero-emissions solution to transportation.

Can You Run Your Gas Car on Water?

While EVs do not use hydrogen or water as fuel, they achieve the same goal of reducing reliance on fossil fuels and decreasing emissions. The growing availability of EVs, combined with advances in battery technology and charging infrastructure, makes them a practical choice for reducing the environmental impact of driving.

Can You Run Your Gas Car on Water?

OUTRO

The idea of running a gas car on water is rooted in the appealing concept of using a clean, abundant resource as fuel. However, the practical challenges of energy inefficiency, hydrogen storage, cost, and safety make it unlikely that water-fueled cars will become a mainstream technology in the near future. While electrolysis can produce hydrogen from water, the energy required to do so far exceeds the energy gained from using hydrogen as a fuel, making it an inefficient and impractical solution.

Instead, alternatives such as hybrid vehicles, hydrogen fuel cells, and electric vehicles offer more viable paths toward reducing fuel consumption and emissions. These technologies are already available and continue to improve, offering practical solutions for a more sustainable transportation future.

In the end, while the dream of running a car on water may remain in the realm of science fiction for now, advancements in clean energy and transportation technologies continue to bring us closer to a world where fossil fuels are no longer the dominant source of power for our vehicles.

ABOUT THE CREATOR

Walter the Educator is one of the pseudonyms for Walter Anderson. Formally educated in Chemistry, Business, and Education, he is an educator, an author, a diverse entrepreneur, and he is the son of a disabled war veteran. "Walter the Educator" shares his time between educating and creating. He holds interests and owns several creative projects that entertain, enlighten, enhance, and educate, hoping to inspire and motivate you. Follow, find new works, and stay up to date with Walter the Educator™

at WaltertheEducator.com

Milton Keynes UK
Ingram Content Group UK Ltd.
UKHW021938281024
450365UK00018B/1152